GREAT PIANO SOLOS

THE SHOW BOOK

CONTENTS

Wise Publications
part of The Music Sales Group
London/New York/Paris/Sydney/Copenhagen/Berlin/Madrid/Tokyo

Published by
Wise Publications
14-15 Berners Street, London W1T 3LJ, UK.

Exclusive Distributors:
Music Sales Limited
Distribution Centre, Newmarket Road,
Bury St Edmunds, Suffolk IP33 3YB, England.

Music Sales Pty Limited
20 Resolution Drive,
Caringbah, NSW 2229, Australia.

Order No. AM982806
ISBN 1-84609-046-6
This book © Copyright 2005 by Wise Publications
a division of Music Sales Limited.

Printed in the EU.

Your Guarantee of Quality:
As publishers, we strive to produce every book to the highest commercial
standards. This book has been carefully designed to minimise awkward
page turns and to make playing from it a real pleasure. Particular care has
been given to specifying acid-free, neutral-sized paper made from pulps
which have not been elemental chlorine bleached. This pulp is from farmed
sustainable forests and was produced with special regard for the
environment. Throughout, the printing and binding have been planned to
ensure a sturdy, attractive publication which should give years of
enjoyment. If your copy fails to meet our high standards, please inform us
and we will gladly replace it.

www.musicsales.com

Anthem
(from "Chess")

Words by Tim Rice, Benny Andersson & Bjorn Ulvaeus
Music by Benny Andersson & Bjorn Ulvaeus

Slow, like a hymn

Another Suitcase In Another Hall
(from "Evita")

Music by Andrew Lloyd Webber
Lyrics by Tim Rice

As If We Never Said Goodbye

(from "Sunset Boulevard")

Music by Andrew Lloyd Webber
Lyrics by Don Black & Christopher Hampton

To Coda ⊕

CODA

10

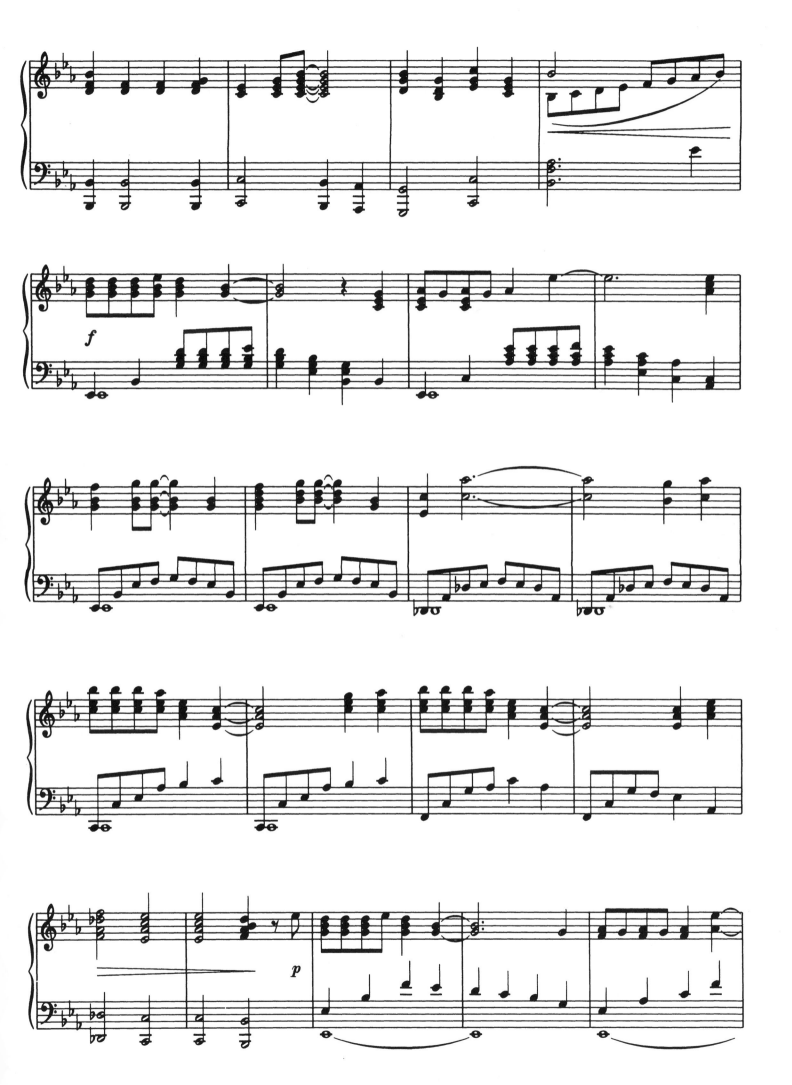

Bali Ha'i
(from "South Pacific")

Words by Oscar Hammerstein II
Music by Richard Rodgers

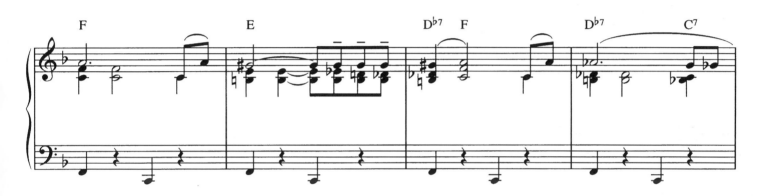

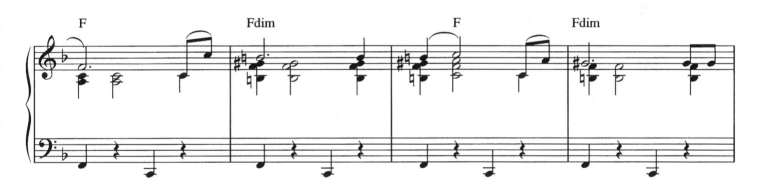

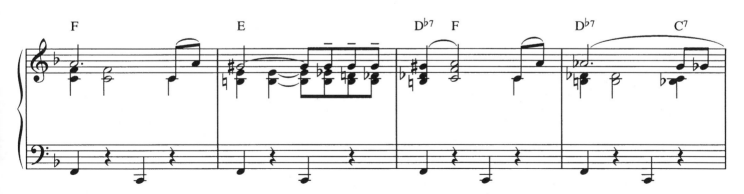

Being Alive
(from "Company")

Words & Music by Stephen Sondheim

Big Spender
(from "Sweet Charity")

Words by Dorothy Fields
Music by Cy Coleman

Aggressively, with swing

Bring Him Home
(from "Les Misérables")

Music by Claude-Michel Schönberg
Lyrics by Alain Boublil & Herbert Kretzmer

Cabaret
(from "Cabaret")

Words by Fred Ebb
Music by John Kander

27

Can't Help Lovin' Dat Man

(from "Show Boat")

Words by Oscar Hammerstein II
Music by Jerome Kern

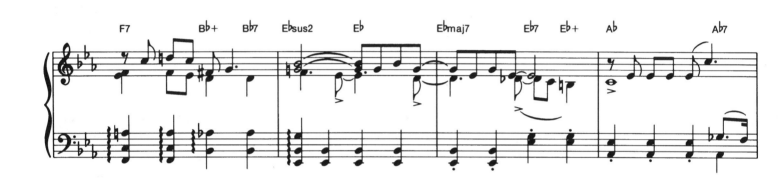

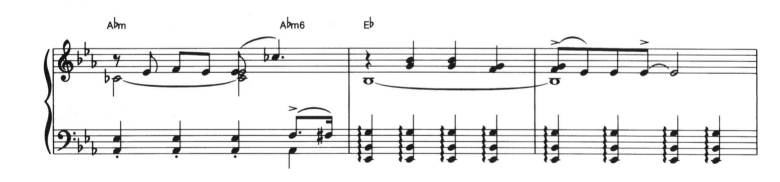

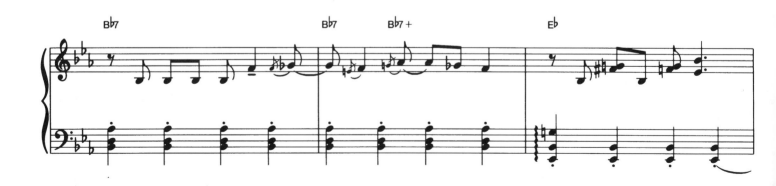

Close Every Door
(from "Joseph And The Amazing Technicolour® Dreamcoat")

Music by Andrew Lloyd Webber
Words by Tim Rice

33

Copacabana (At The Copa)
(from "Copacabana")

Words & Music by Barry Manilow, Bruce Sussman & Jack Feldman

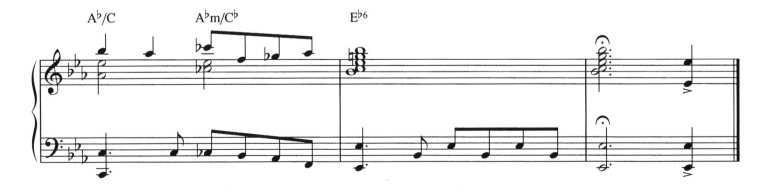

Diamonds Are A Girl's Best Friend

(from "Gentlemen Prefer Blondes")

Words by Leo Robin
Music by Jule Styne

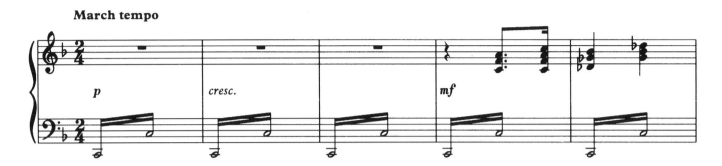

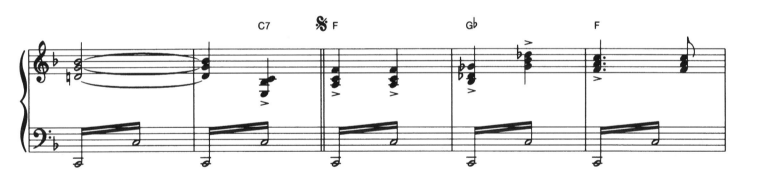

Do-Re-Mi
(from "The Sound Of Music")

Words by Oscar Hammerstein II
Music by Richard Rodgers

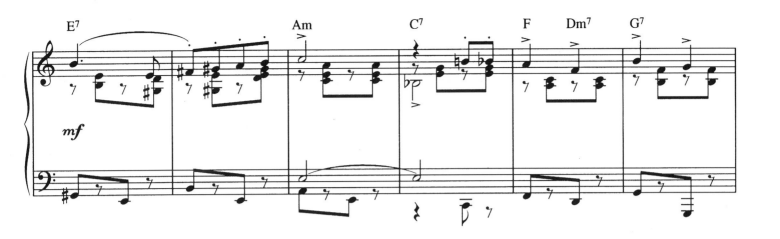

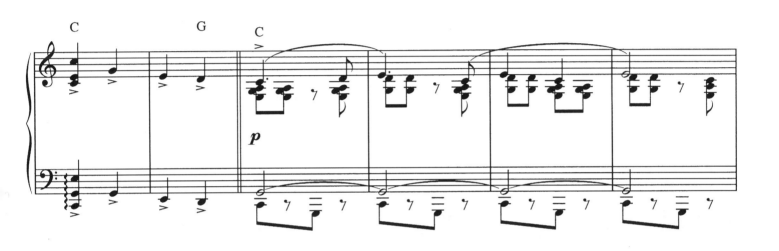

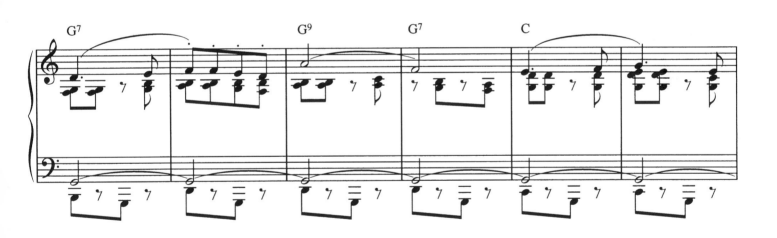

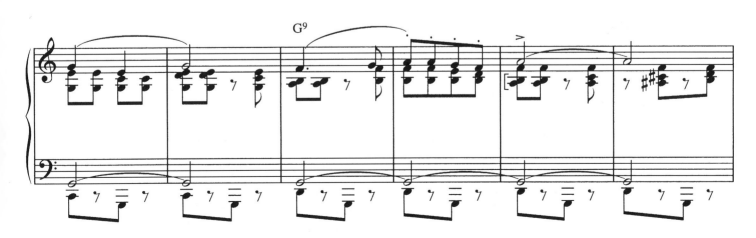

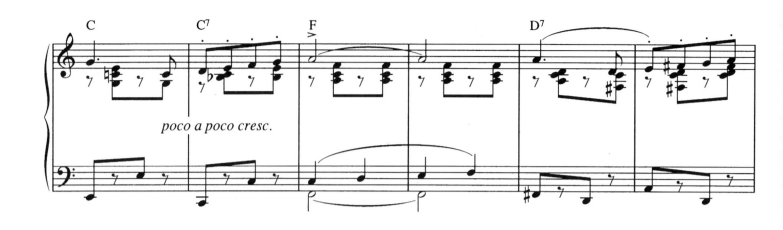

poco a poco cresc.

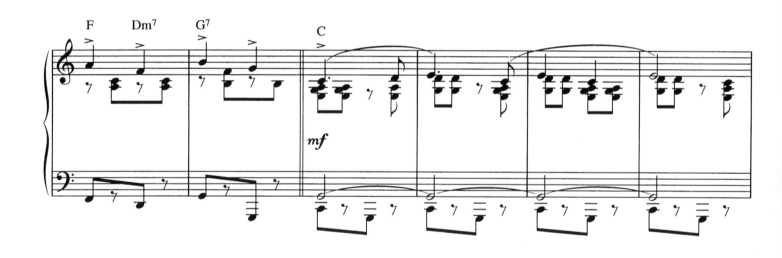

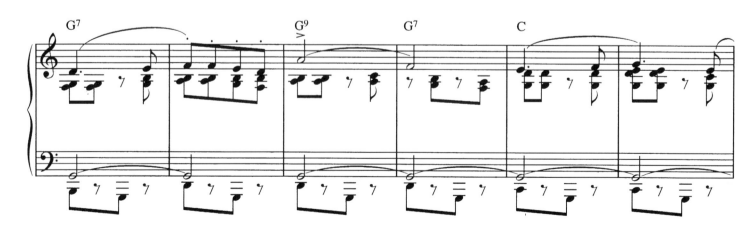

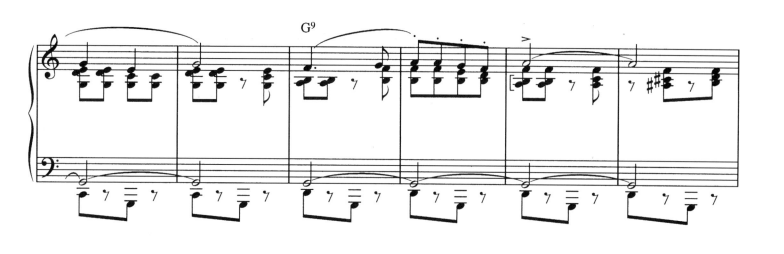

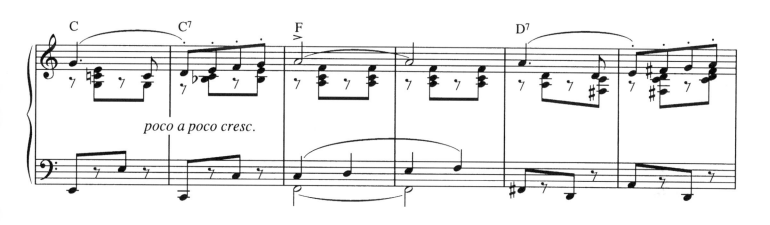

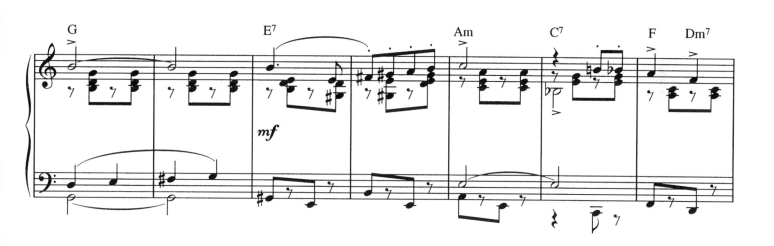

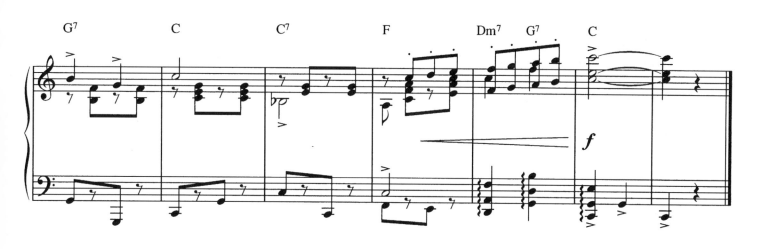

Don't Cry For Me Argentina
(from "Evita")

Music by Andrew Lloyd Webber
Words by Tim Rice

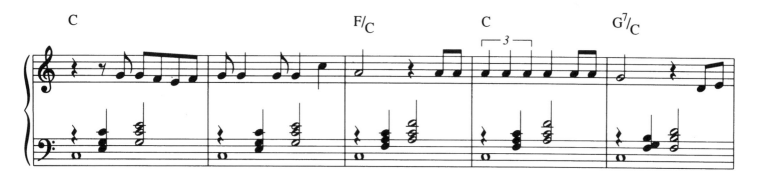

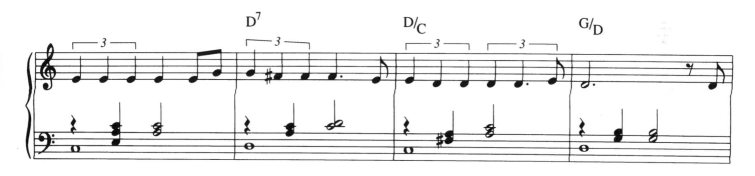

Slow Tango

49

Empty Chairs At Empty Tables
(from "Les Misérables")

Music by Claude-Michel Schönberg
Lyrics by Alain Boublil & Herbert Kretzmer

Moderately slow

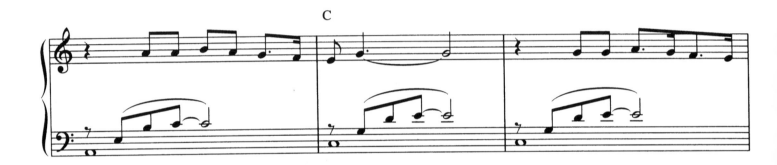

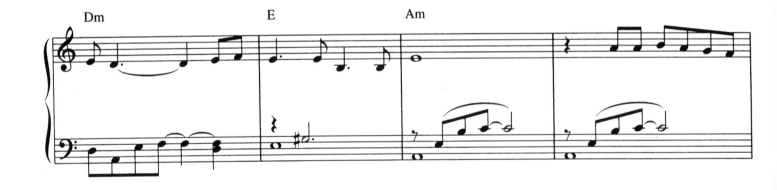

Hopelessly Devoted To You

(from "Grease")

Words & Music by John Farrar

I Dreamed A Dream
(from "Les Misérables")

Music by Claude-Michel Schönberg
Original Lyrics by Alain Boublil & Jean-Marc Natel
English Lyrics by Herbert Kretzmer

59

I Don't Know How To Love Him

(from "Jesus Christ Superstar")

Music by Andrew Lloyd Webber
Words by Tim Rice

I Know Him So Well
(from "Chess")

Words by Tim Rice and Bjorn Ulvaeus
Music by Benny Andersson and Bjorn Ulvaeus

I Whistle A Happy Tune
(from "The King And I")

Words by Oscar Hammerstein II
Music by Richard Rodgers

I'll Never Fall In Love Again

(from "Promises, Promises")

Words by Hal David
Music by Burt Bacharach

If I Were A Rich Man

(from "Fiddler On The Roof")

Words by Sheldon Harnick
Music by Jerry Bock

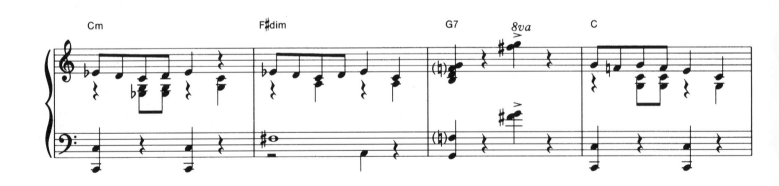

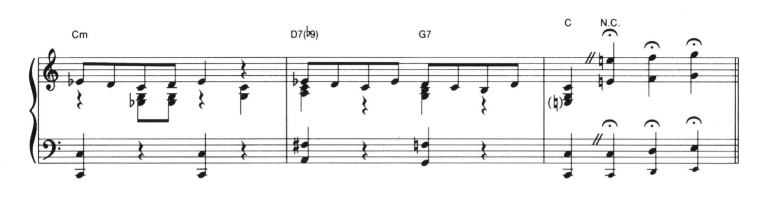

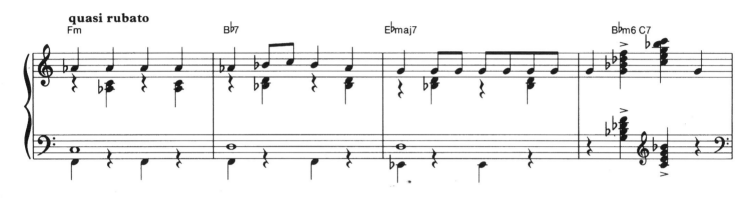

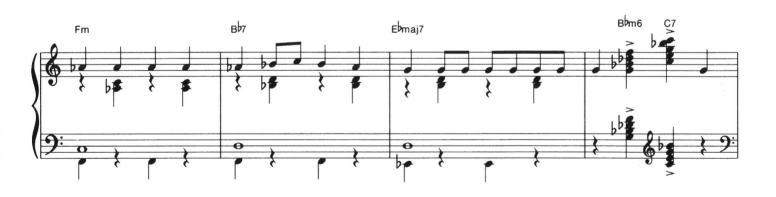

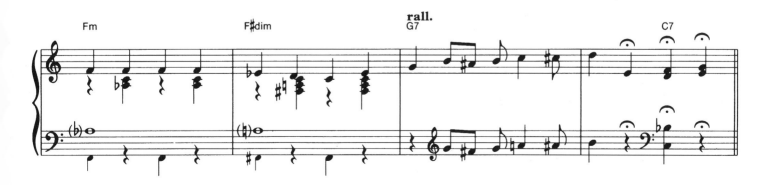

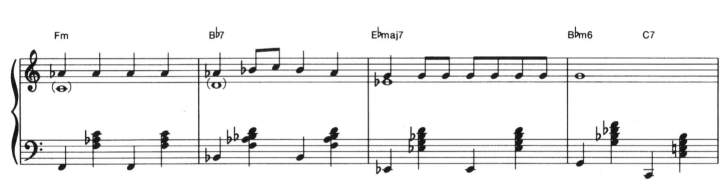

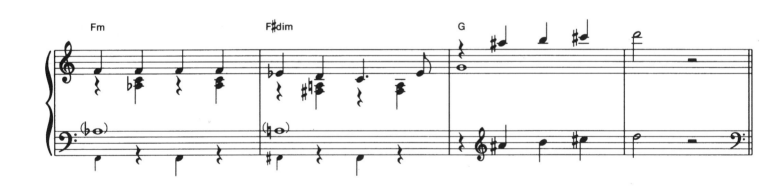

If My Friends Could See Me Now

(from "Sweet Charity")

Words by Dorothy Fields
Music by Cy Coleman

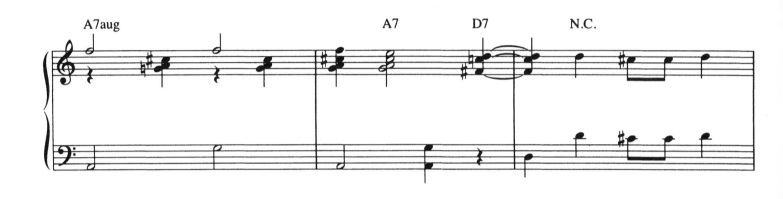

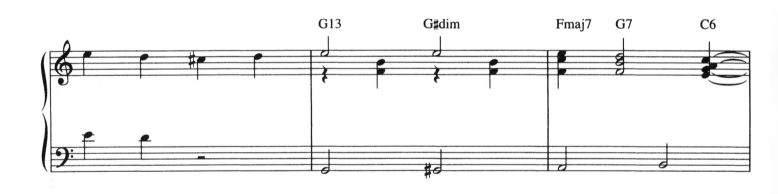

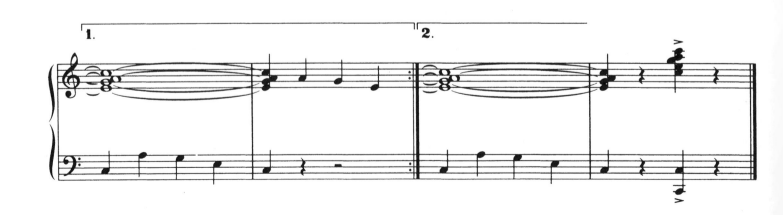

Is You Is Or Is You Ain't My Baby?

(from "Five Guys Named Moe")

Words & Music by Billy Austin & Louis Jordan

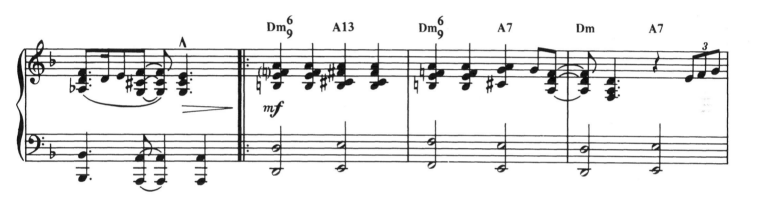

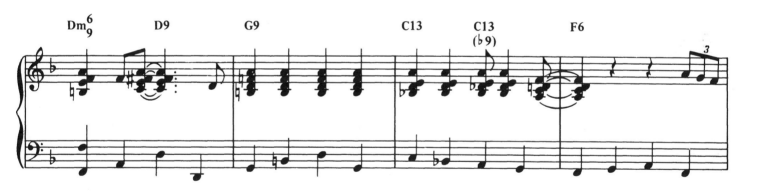

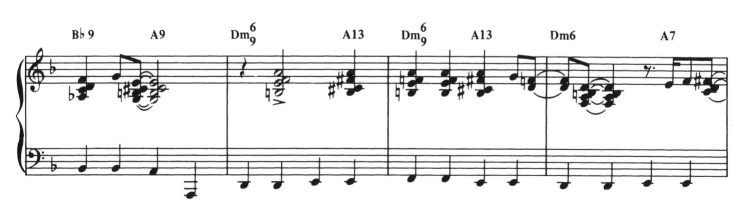

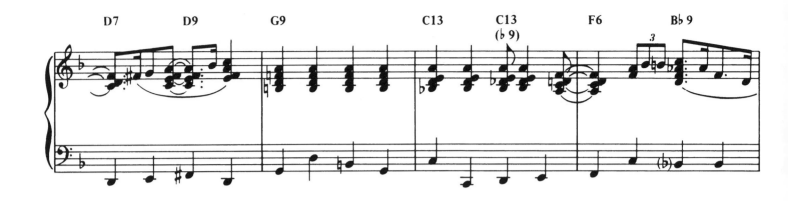

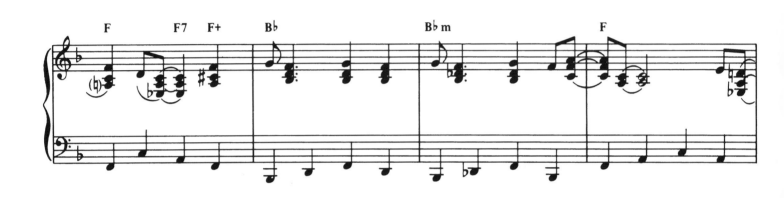

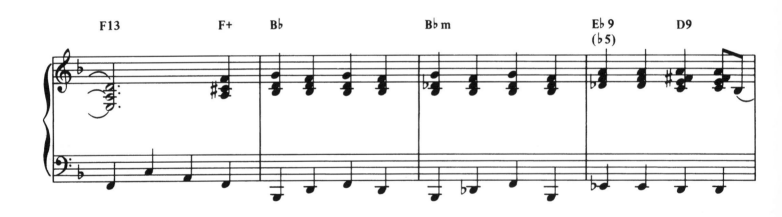

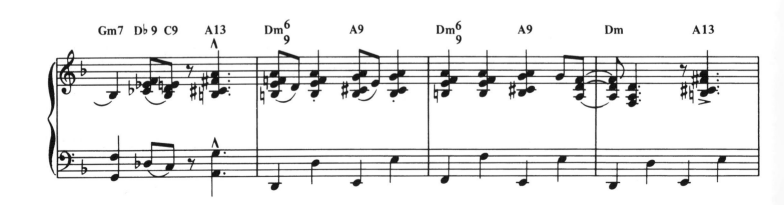

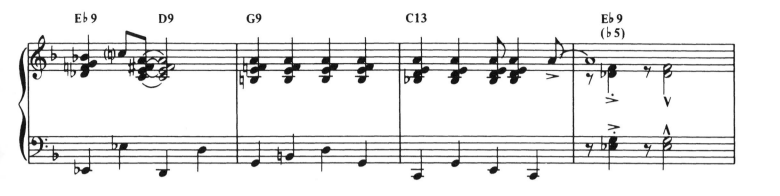

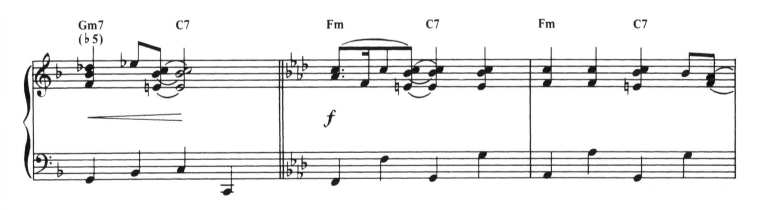

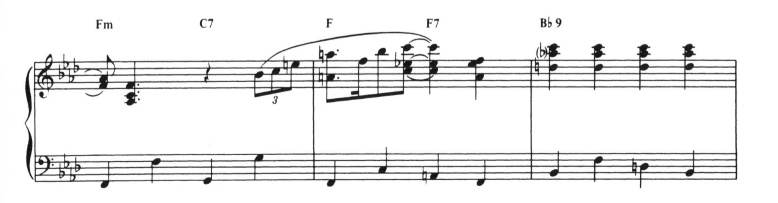

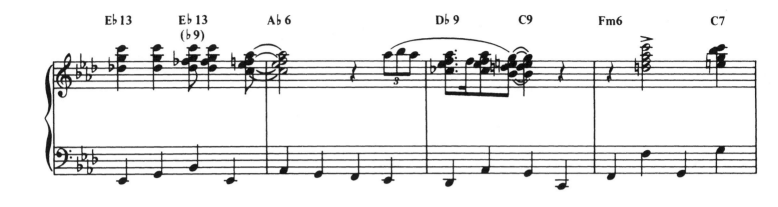

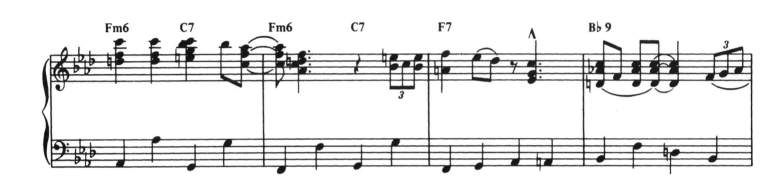

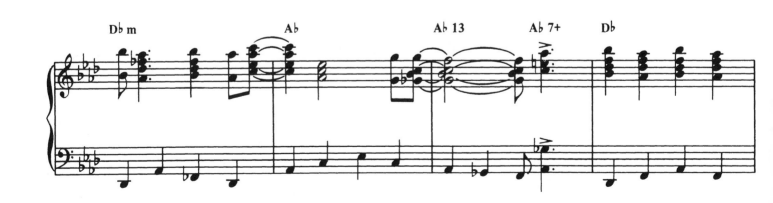

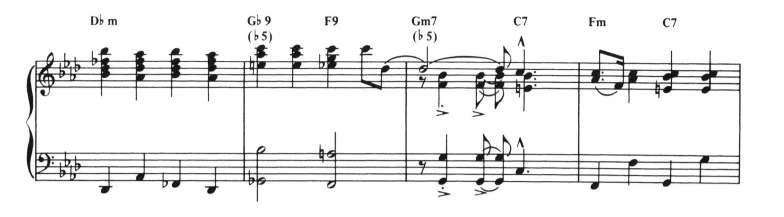

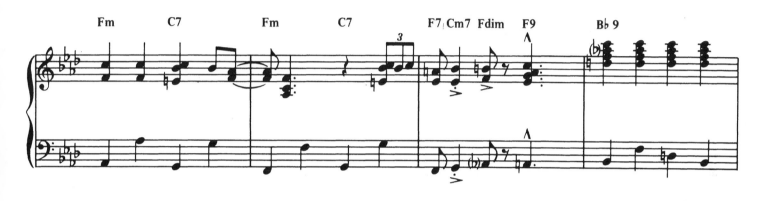

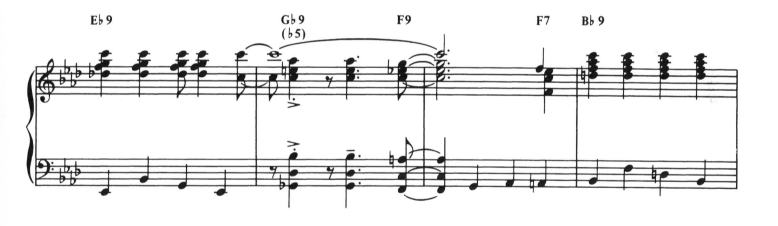

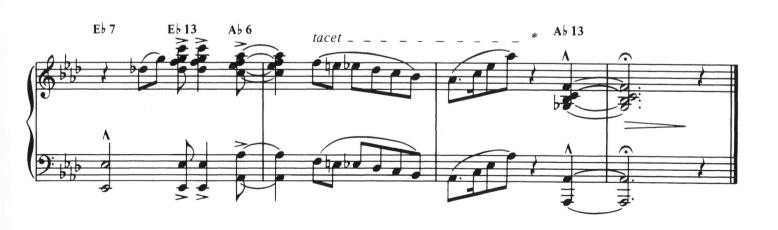

Luck Be A Lady
(from "Guys And Dolls")

Words & Music by Frank Loesser

Memory
(from "Cats")

Music by Andrew Lloyd Webber
Words by Trevor Nunn after T.S. Eliot

93

Now That I've Seen Her (Her Or Me)

(from "Miss Saigon")

Words by Alain Boublil & Richard Maltby Jr.
Music by Claude-Michel Schönberg

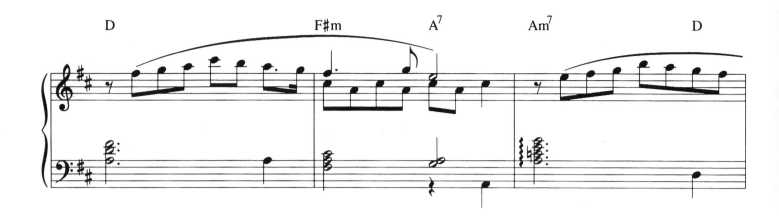

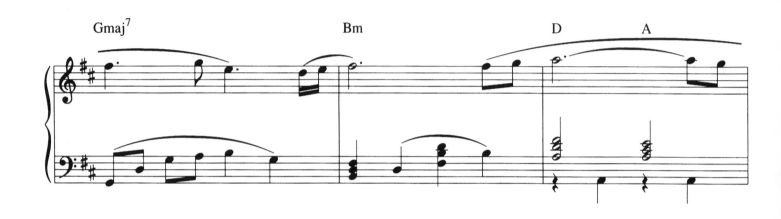

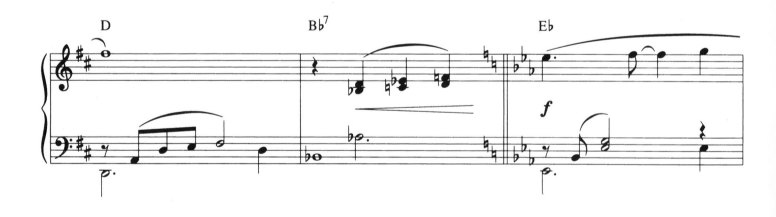

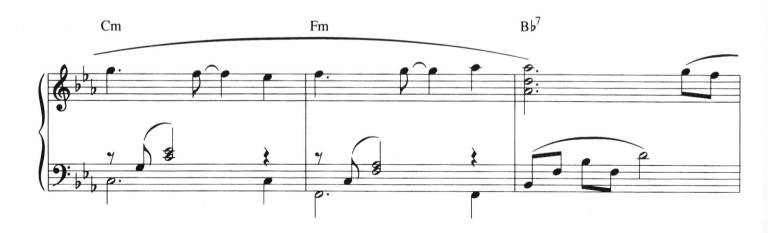

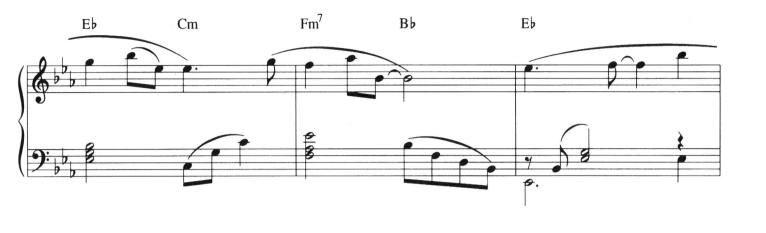

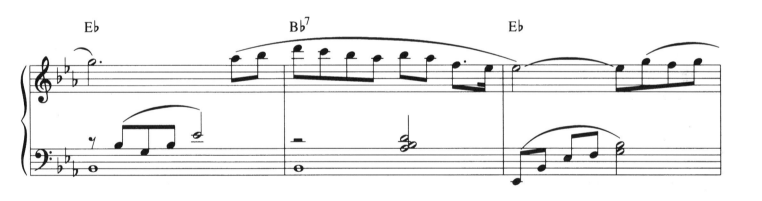

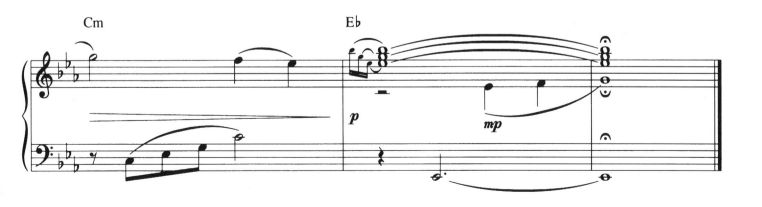

The Music Of The Night
(from "The Phantom Of The Opera")

Music by Andrew Lloyd Webber
Words by Charles Hart

Andante, with expression

101

No Matter What
(from "Whistle Down The Wind")

Music by Andrew Lloyd Webber
Lyrics by Jim Steinman

Moderately

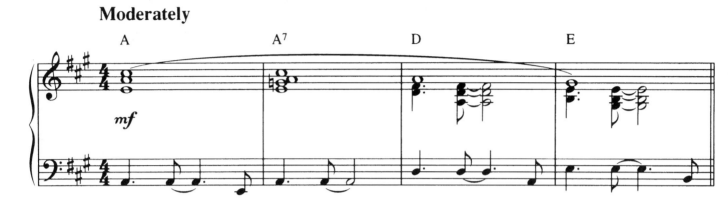

Ol' Man River
(from "Show Boat")

Words by Oscar Hammerstein II
Music by Jerome Kern

On My Own
(from "Les Misérables")

Music by Claude-Michel Schönberg
Original Lyrics by Alain Boublil & Jean-Marc Natel
English Lyrics by Herbert Kretzmer, Trevor Nunn & John Caird

113

One

(from "A Chorus Line")

Words by Edward Kleban
Music by Marvin Hamlisch

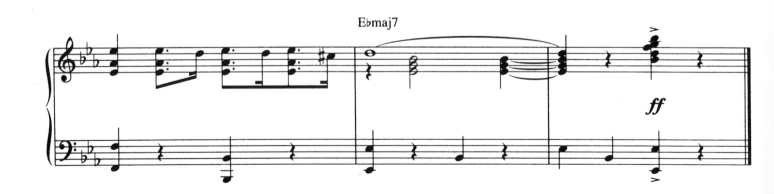

Smoke Gets In Your Eyes

(from "Roberta")

Words by Otto Harbach
Music by Jerome Kern

Pick A Pocket Or Two
(from "Oliver!")

Words & Music by Lionel Bart

Some Enchanted Evening
(from "South Pacific")

Words by Oscar Hammerstein II
Music by Richard Rodgers

Sunrise, Sunset

(from "Fiddler On The Roof")

Words by Sheldon Harnick
Music by Jerry Bock

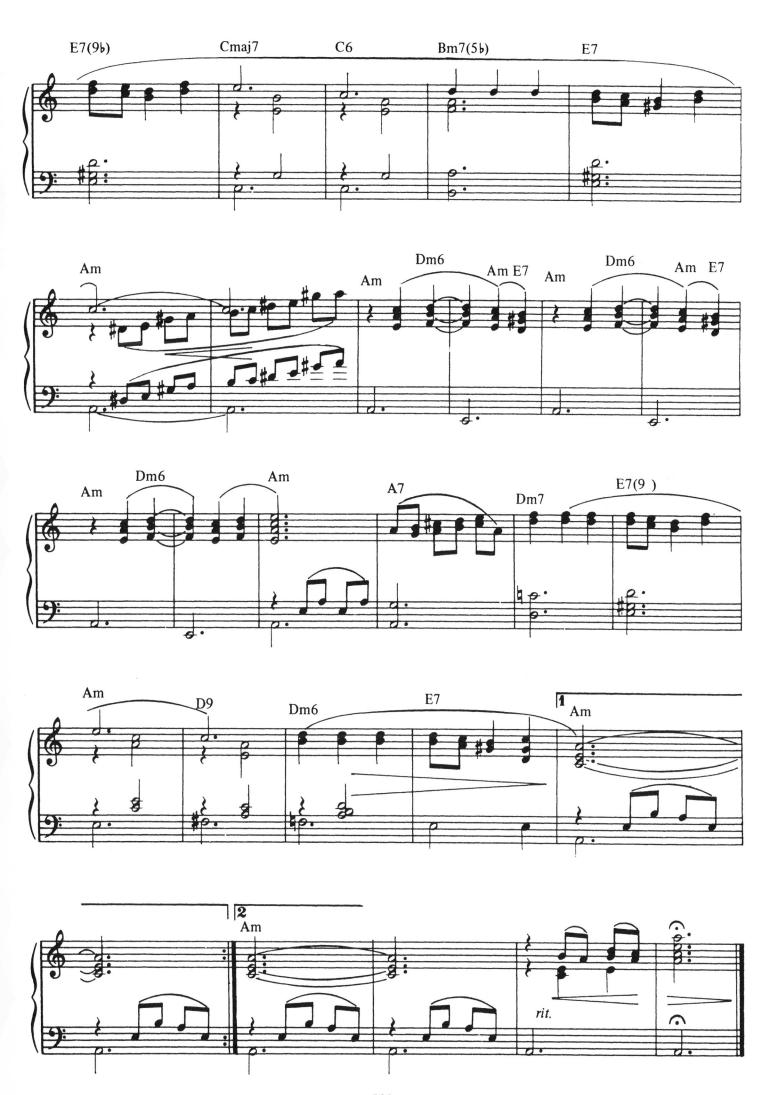

Starlight Express
(from "Starlight Express")

Music by Andrew Lloyd Webber
Words by Richard Stilgoe

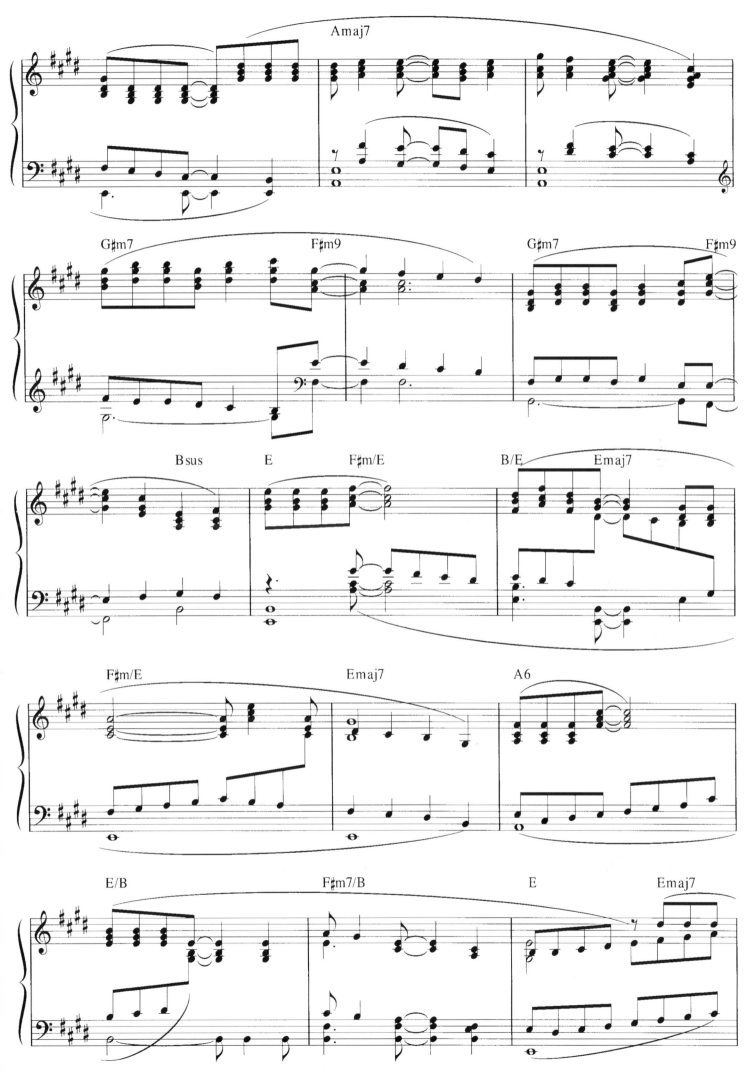

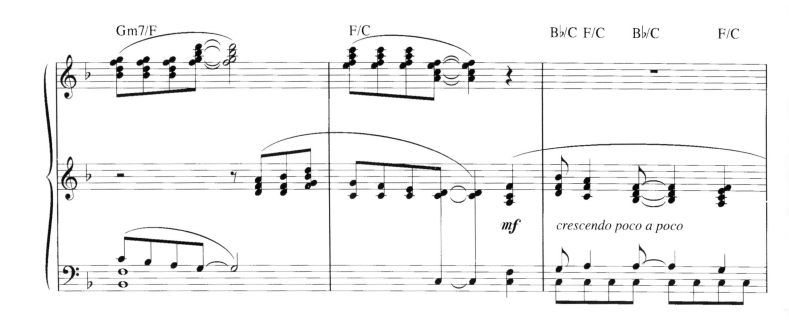

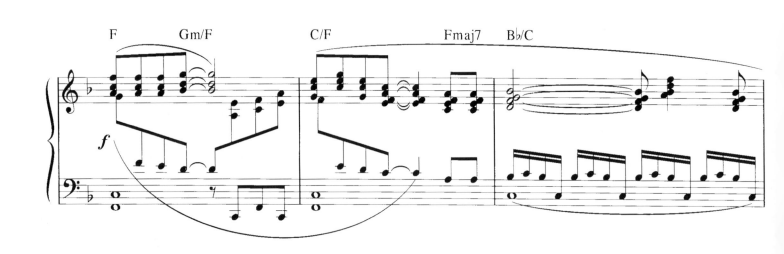

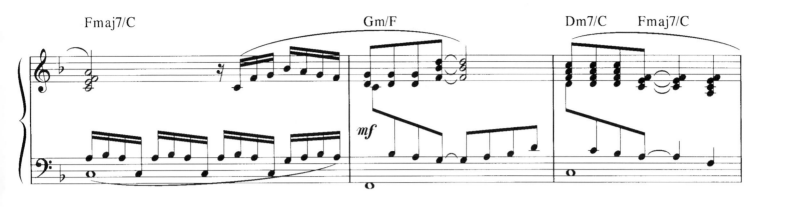

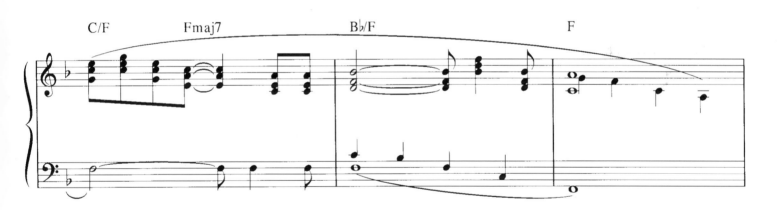

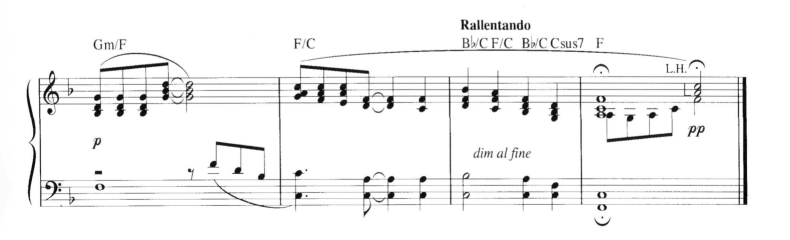

Sun And Moon
(from "Miss Saigon")

Music by Claude-Michel Schönberg
Lyrics by Alain Boublil & Richard Maltby Jr.
Adapted from original French Lyrics by Alain Boublil

Moderately

More movement

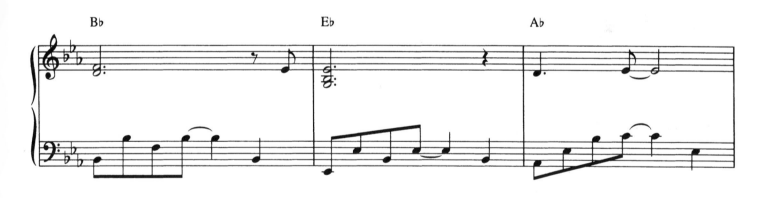

Take That Look Off Your Face
(from "Tell Me On A Sunday")

Music by Andrew Lloyd Webber
Words by Don Black

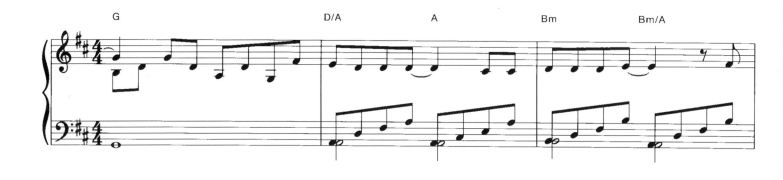

Tell Me It's Not True
(from "Blood Brothers")

Words & Music by Willy Russell

Till There Was You
(from "The Music Man")

Words & Music by Meredith Willson

Willkommen
(from "Cabaret")

Words by Fred Ebb
Music by John Kander

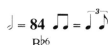

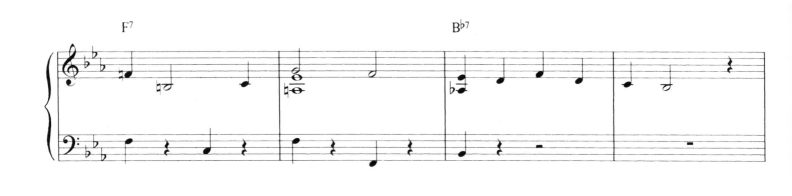

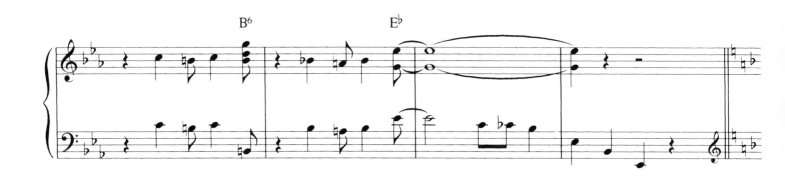

Slower

Wishing You Were Somehow Here Again

(from "The Phantom Of The Opera")

Music by Andrew Lloyd Webber
Words by Charles Hart

You'll Never Walk Alone
(from "Carousel")

Words by Oscar Hammerstein II
Music by Richard Rodgers

Moderately

Thank You For The Music
(from "Mamma Mia!")

Words & Music by Benny Andersson & Bjorn Ulvaeus

160